MICHAEL POWELL`S

THE EDGE OF THE W

Then & Now

DAVID W EARL

ISBN: 978-09523928-5-9

HANOVER PUBLICATIONS

CONTENTS

Acknowledgements, Bibliography & Sources........ 5
Introduction........ 6
Film Synopsis........ 11
Cast & Crew List........ 13
The People of Foula........ 14
The Director—Michael Powell 15
Location photos—Then & Now........ 17
Foula Map & Scene Locations........ 68
Shetland children & Scottish players in the movie........ 69
Foula folk in the Edge of the World........ 70
Cast & Crew biographies 78
Sailing vessels used in the movie........ 100
Powell`s Ark........ 103

Front Cover: Belle Chrystall & Niall MacGinnis in a scene from `*The Edge of the World*` a colourized version of a production still from the estate of Michael Powell.

Rear Cover: Film strip with then & now photos : Estate of Michael Powell and Author. Foula Isle Photo`s: David Ramsey. Lerwick harbour: Photo: Author.

ACKNOWLEDGEMENTS

First of all I must thank posthumously, the great British film director Michael Powell. Had it not been for his conceivable idea that such a movie could ever be made under such conditions in the first place, and his persistence and determination to get the job done in the first half of the 20th Century, then I would not be writing this book in the 21st Century.

Next, I must thank all the people who helped or inspired me to make this work possible:
Isobel Holbourn, John Holbourn, Eric Isbister, Edith Gray, Dave Ramsey, Geoff Bland, Kevin Gear, Bryan Taylor, Sheila Gear, Margaret Pitt (Nee Greig), Thelma Schoomaker, Steve Crook, Columba Powell, Fiona Williams, Lindsey Bender, Donna Atherton, Jeff Atherton, Capt Marshall Wishart, Capt Hughie Manson, Brian Rose and of course the late great British film director Michael Powell.

Organizations:

My grateful thanks to the following: Foula Heritage, Berlin Associates, The British Film Institute, The Estate of Michael Powell, Shetland Tourist Board, Ordnance Survey.

Photographs:

All B/W stills from the film Michael Powell`s *`The Edge of the World`* are courtesy of the Estate of Michael Powell and the British Film Foundation and permission has been granted for use in this publication. Also I am most grateful to Mr Powell`s widow Thelma Schoonmaker for her influence making this possible. Colour photo`s are by the author unless stated otherwise.

Bibliography and Sources:

200,000 Feet on Foula. Michael Powell. Faber & Faber, 1938.
Michael Powell - A Life in Movies - An Autobiography. Mandarin 1992
Michael Powell - Million Dollar Movie, Random House Inc 1995
The Edge of the World. 1937 Joe Rock Productions. BFI DVD 2004.
Foula - Island West of the Sun. Sheila Gear. Robert Hale Ltd. 1983.
The Scotsman newspapers 1936-38.

INTRODUCTION

During 2003 I began researching on a couple of aircraft that had crashed on the Island of Foula in the Shetland group in the Second World War. Further research led me to a number of books in order to seek out the geographical locations. Also, a film produced by British director Michael Powell entitled *`The Edge of the World`* released in 1937 was viewed and I became more and more intrigued by this tiny island and its inhabitants.

More interest in both the aircraft and the movie inspired me to make plans for a trip to this island, which was still by no means an easy task even in this day and age. Foula lies some 20 miles west of the Shetland Mainland, and at a latitude of 60 degrees, stretches as far north as the southern tip of Greenland. Getting there from my hometown of Stalybridge near Manchester would take three aircraft and a lot of luck with the weather.

May 2006 - Having flown to Sumburgh in foul weather with a couple of companions Dave Ramsey and Geoff Bland, via a short stop at Edinburgh and Wick in Caithness, we finally landed at Sumburgh in the Shetland Isles in bright blue skies and sunshine. A few days were spent on the largest Island known as Mainland where the scenes with the fishing fleet and the climb sequence boats were filmed. Then on the morning of the 24th we departed from Tingwall airstrip in a Loganair Britten Norman Islander bound for Foula.

Capt Marshall Wishart was our pilot, and with a smooth flight, we had fantastic views across the islands. Soon the heights of Hamnafield hill, the crofts of South Biggins and the old ruined Kirk came into view, as did the magnificent sea cliffs of the Kame and Wester Hoevdi and rocky coastline at Hellibrek and South Ness.

As we touched down on the gravel runway, built incidentally by the island folk themselves, we were soon greeted by the Island`s ranger Isobel Holbourn, whom we had planned to stay with for a few days in her self catering cottage at Ristie. This was an old converted croft house on the north side of the isle close to the Gaada Stack, a unique triple stone arch and memorable setting for several of the movie scenes. On arrival at Ristie and wanting to make the most the splendid weather, we set off for the hills straight away. We were soon aloft Hamnafield and greeted by a magnificent panorama. I just stood in awe of the view. ` What a fantastic place!`.

Visits were made with many of the local folk regarding the aircraft, the film, and life on Foula in general. Eric Isbister told us of the Whitley bomber that came down in April 1943 near his house at South Biggins. Jim Gear of Magdala told us of his father`s involvement in the rescue of an airman from the blazing wreck of a Canso flying boat in July 1944.

Steve Smith then of North Harrier, took us around the various sites of old crofts, and Edith Gray of Dykes, who was an extra in the movie *`The Edge of the World`,* told us of her involvement in the making of the film and life on the island. In fact it was this visit with Edith that prompted more interest in the movie and my quest to glean more information on the locations used by Mr Powell. Also I wanted to learn more about Island folk who were involved with the making of the film, both as extras, and the various chores to do with the production.

The time spent on this tiny Isle was a time I`ll never forget. Walking the hills of Soberlie, Da Sneug, Da Noup and Hamnafield, seeing the old Kirk used in some of the first scenes of Mr Powell`s movie, and the pier where in 1936 locals had gathered for the Lairds visit and the big evacuation scene.

Those glorious few days bathed in blue skies and warm sunshine had alas passed all too quickly, and I knew before the aircraft left the runway that I would have to return. Foula had indeed cast its spell on me.

The following year, I heard of a book written by Michael Powell on the making of his movie entitled *`200,000 Feet on Foula`* (Referring to the amount of film used in the production) I managed to get hold of a copy from a bookshop in Connecticut, USA, it took around a month to arrive but when it did, I read it cover to cover and was totally captivated by Mr Powell`s attention to detail. He described with perfection the difficulties of each location, the problems with light, sound, and the wild weather they were to encounter during the 16 weeks of filming from June to October in 1936.

He described local folk used as extras in the film almost as if he`d known them all his life, for example in the scene where `Ruth` (Belle Chrystall) with her new born baby (Margaret Greig) in a cradle, soon to be followed by the dance sequence with fiddlers playing `Da Foula Reel` he says :

"The scene of the most ambitious sequence in the film was Sloag, a thatched croft in the brae north of the Haa............I had two big sequences there, the Lullaby scene and the Foula Reel.

The Lullaby opens with a shot over the sea, white pools of light are falling from a stormy sky and waving grass is in the foreground. The camera starts to swing, round past the fields, over a field of oats bent by the wind, black and white and uneasy like the sea, round and farther round until a wooden cradle appears amongst the corn and the camera stops on a close up of the baby asleep.

The cradle gently rocking. Belle is seen, bent over it, with the Dumplings (The film crew nick-name for the Gray Sisters Nanny and Jenny of a croft named Stoel) *and others around her. In the distance Hamish plays the violin. The hills are black against the setting sun. The wind blows the smoke of the chimneys out in a long ribbon.*

Other people are arriving. It is an unofficial gathering as the light fails. The elder women sit busily knitting in a row under the corn. Mrs Isbister`s gentle face; Mrs Gray`s firm one; Mrs Henry`s square old jaw on her worn hand. Tommy Gray listens solemnly, the `Archdeacon`* ( Film crew name for old Robert Isbister) *fills his pipe, old John Gray puffs away composedly (He`s paid to do it mind you!), Robbie leans challengingly against the door at Brae.

Out of the shadows walk Finlay and John Laurie. It is evidently the first official visit to his granddaughter ....`

While music on the violin by Hamish Sutherland and voices of the women of the Glasgow Orpheus Choir fill the air, the camera swiftly cuts to the dance sequence, described in Powell`s book as follows:

`In a flash the scene changes. Night has fallen, lanterns are lit, there is dancing on the green. Hamish leads a dashing group of fiddlers in the Foula Reel. Wullie Gear is hitting it hot and strong. Jimmy O` the Shop is striking sparks. Peter Ratter lacks fire but makes the grade...............Now the Foula Reel is being danced. Down the row of clapping hands gallops a bearded, sprightly figure, spurning the grass in a way to shame the even younger generation. An amazing beret crowns his head, a bulky jersey cover a giant torso, his hand in his slender partner`s - Maggie Jean from Skeld, on a visit to her cousin at Punds. In other words John Opens the dance`.

Though the majority of the film was shot on Foula, all the fishing boat scenes were done in Lerwick, with the exception of the trawler used in the evacuation that was filmed off Scalloway.

Though the climb was done on Foula, near the Sneck, the boats in the climb sequence for various reasons had to be left until last. In fact they left the isle not having filmed it, fortunately it was done later at the Knab near Lerwick, Shetland.

Having been inspired greatly by both the book and the movie, during winter 2007 I began preparations for a return trip to Foula. This time a full week would be spent on the island, and a week on the Shetland mainland talking to locals, taking film footage and photographing the various locations used in the 1937 production.

On Saturday 17th May 2008 at 8.50am, I boarded flight BE 7222 a Brazilian built Embraer 145 jet at Manchester bound for Edinburgh. It was to be a smooth trip that took just a little over forty five minutes. Only one of my earlier companions Geoff Bland, would accompany me on this expedition and it was planned to meet up with him in Lerwick that evening.

Having transferred to another aircraft at Edinburgh, the journey would continue via British Airways SAAB Turbo-prop, flight BE 8993 taking just 90 minutes to reach Sumburgh, Shetland, and despite a rather turbulent journey in squally conditions, the plane finally touched down in glorious sunshine which was to last throughout the whole trip.

Much time was spent throughout our trip, speaking to locals, walking the hills, the coastline, lochs and valleys, photographing and filming just about anything and everything. As luck would have it, not only did we get to take a trip around the island in the old ex-lifeboat and mail boat *Westering Homewards* owned by Bryan Taylor of Leraback, but we also got a circuit of the isle by air on the way home thanks to our pilot Capt Hughie Manson. Also a trip to Scalloway, Shetland, courtesy of Jim Manson of Forth Charlotte Guest House in Lerwick who was kind enough to provide us with a vehicle.

All in all a fantastic time on this wonderful island was had on both occasions and I would like to thank the people from the bottom of my heart for all the time they gave us on our visit.

David W. Earl
Stalybridge,
Cheshire. 2014

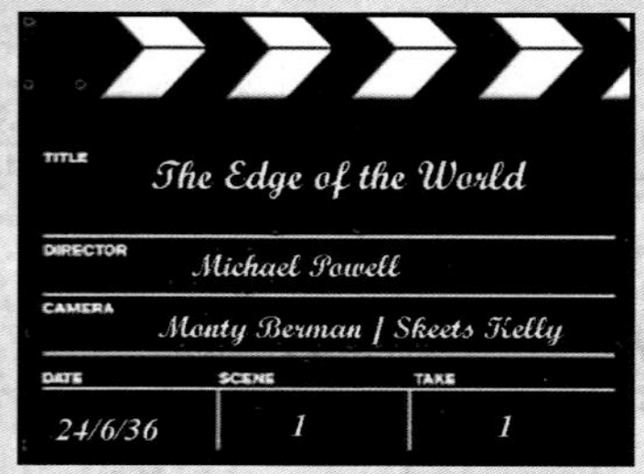

THE EDGE OF THE WORLD

"It started out just a film, but became an experience that changed all our lives"

John Laurie: ***Return to the Edge of the World 1978***

FILM SYNOPSIS

The opening title sequence itself explains much of what the film is about and begins:

The slow shadow of death is falling on the outer islands of Scotland. This is the story of one of them—and all of them. When the Roman fleet first sailed round Britain, they saw from the Orkneys,* a distant island. Like a blue haze across a hundred miles of sea.
They called it —
"ULITMA THULE"

THE EDGE OF THE WORLD.

The movie begins with the arrival of a yacht round the cliffs of Foula (or Hirta as it is called in the film) The occupants, a Mr & Mrs Graham and a crewman Andrew Gray, a former inhabitant of the isle. The trio land at the old pier and wander around the deserted crofts before heading for the cliffs.

Andrew encounters a stone tablet at the edge of a precipice; it reads, `PETER MANSON ..GONE OVER.` Mr Graham remarks "*Does it mean, gone over there?*" "*Many died that way*" says Andrew, "*Hunting for eggs or after the sheep, sooner or later a rope frayed or a foot slipped, it became a word for death on the island*". "*A nasty looking place!*" Remarks Mr Graham. "*Aye, it is!*" Says Andrew as he lifts his head and glances towards the Scottish Mainland. "*What`s wrong Andrew?*" asks Graham, "*The hills of Scotland .....Local folk used to say.........*" He pauses, "*What?*" "*That it was bad luck to see the hills*"

Andrew knows all too well the story of the stone and begins to tell the tale.....

"*It`s the Sabbath today, and a fine summer morning. Ten years ago you`d have seen all the folk on the way to the Kirk. The men in black and the women neat and bonnie, and young John Isbister standing by the gate. The bell would be ringing.......*"

It was said that trawlers overfishing had threatened the survival of the inhabitants as a fishing community, and to add to this younger members of the population were seeking better lives elsewhere, but elder Peter Manson, (John Laurie) one of the Isle`s leaders, does his utmost to resist evacuation to the mainland, though his son Robbie, (Eric Berry) just back from making good money over there has his own ideas and is making plans to leave the island himself and marry a girl over there.

Meanwhile, Robbie's sister Ruth (Belle Chrystall) plans to marry his best friend, Andrew Gray (Niall MacGinnis) and stay on the island. Andrew and Robbie argue over the island`s future and decide to settle the matter the way they did in the old days, by a race to the top of the cliff at Westa Hoevdi, the victor having the final say on the matter. Ruth is terrified, fearing she may lose them both and her fears are brought to a startling reality when the race ends in tragedy, which tears apart the families of Manson and Gray.

Time passes and Ruth reveals she is pregnant, which at first angers her father Peter Manson. However, he realizes that this might just bring the two families back together, but not before further trouble and desperation hits the islanders.

The story of the island struggling to make a living is based on the real life events that Michael had read about in the national press, which had occurred on St.kilda (Hirta) in Scotland`s Outer Hebrides, leading to its eventual evacuation in 1930. He decided there and then that one day he would make a film about this, though his original plans to make it on the island of St.Kilda were rejected by Lord Dumfries, the owner of the isle, on account that the production would disturb the birds.

Not to be beaten, Michael with a budget of £20,000 for the whole movie, set about finding an alternative location and an island of similar proportion, a mammoth task yet it took much less time than anyone anticipated, save for Michael of course who had every confidence he would find such a location. Eventually Foula was discovered and after some negotiating the Holbourn family, owners of the isle, gave their permission to film there for the princely sum of £200 an equivalent today of almost £12,000.

The film is a must for all island lovers. The dramatic locations, breath-taking scenery and excellent cinematography and music score make it all the more enjoyable.

* `The Orkneys` : A term describing the archipelago consisting approx 70 islands 10 miles (16km) north of Caithness, Scotland, is referred to these days quite simply as Orkney. The former is seldom used now except by some visitors, and locals much prefer the term Orkney.
.

CAST & CREW

PETER MANSON .... JOHN LAURIE
JAMES GRAY .... FINLAY CURRIE
ANDREW GRAY .... NIALL MacGINNIS
RUTH MANSON .... BELLE CHRYSTALL
ROBBIE MANSON .... ERIC BERRY
JOHN ISBISTER THE CATECHIST GRANT SUTHERLAND
JEAN MANSON ....KITTY KIRWAN
THE LAIRD—MR DUNBAR.............CAMPBELL ROBSON
TRAWLER SKIPPER McPHEE........ GEORGE SUMMERS
Dr INKSTER .... JIM GARRIOCK
MR GRAHAM......................................MICHAEL POWELL
MRS GRAHAM .... FRANKIE REIDY

WRITTEN & DIRECTED BY............MICHAEL POWELL

MUSICAL DIRECTOR .... CYRIL RAY
CHORAL EFFECTS .... WOMEN OF THE GLASGOW ORPHEUS CHOIR
CONDUCTOR .... SIR HUGH ROBERTSON
ORCHESTRATIONS .... W. LAMBERT WILLIAMSON

CAMERAS .... ERNEST PALMER
SKEETS KELLY
MONTY BERMAN

CAMERA ASSISTANT................JOHN BEHR

PRODUCER ....JOE ROCK

PRODUCTION STAFF .... GERALD BLATTNER
JOHN A. SEABOURNE
VERNON A.SEWELL
W .H .FARR
GEORGE BLACK Jr
BILL PATON

CHIEF OF CONSTRUCTION ....SIDNEY S. STREETER

EDITOR ....DEREK TWIST
ASSISTANT EDITOR ....BOB WALTERS
SOUND ....LIONEL K. TREGELLAS
SOUND ASSISTANTS........................LEN & BILL MARTIN
PROPS .... WILLIAM OSBORNE
RECORDING ENGINEER.................BILL H.O. SWEENY

SHETLAND & FOULA FOLK WITH UNCREDITED ROLES

JAMES ANDREW ....GERALD UMPHRAY
GIRL WITH KITTENS .... JESSAMINE SMITH
THE BABY .... MARGARET GREIG
BOY AT FOULA REEL ....ALFRED ISBISTER
GIRL AT FOULA REEL ....STELLA SUTHERLAND

THE PEOPLE OF FOULA

The following are known to have appeared as extras in the film and assisted the production staff.

ANDY GEAR - Schoolhouse
HARRY GEAR - Mogle
JEMIMA `Mima` GEAR - Mogle
CHRISTINA `Tina`GEAR - Mogle
PETER GEAR - Mogle
WILLIAM `Wullie` GEAR - Mogle
AGNES GRAY - Stoel
ANDREW GRAY - North Harrier
EDITH GRAY - Dykes
JAMES ANDREW `Jimmy` GRAY - Dykes
JEAN GRAY - Dykes
JOHN GRAY - Burns
LOUISA `Louie` GRAY - Dykes
THOMAS `Tammie` GRAY - Dykes
PETER GRAY - Burns
MURIEL GRAY - Burns
AGNES JANE `Aggie Jean` ISBISTER - South Biggins
ALFRED ISBISTER - South Biggins
GEORGE `Dodie` ISBISTER - Leraback
JAMES `Jimmy` ISBISTER - South Biggins
IVOR ISBISTER - South Biggins
ELIZABETH `Lizzie` ISBISTER - Ham
ROBERT `Bobby` ISBISTER - South Biggins
ROBERT W `Robbie` ISBISTER - South Biggins
BESSIE HENRY - North Biggins
JAMES HENRY - Quenister
JESSIE HENRY - North Biggins
JAMES `Jimmy` HENRY - Niggards
MARGARET `Maggie` HENRY - North Biggins
MAGNUS `Magnie` HENRY - North Biggins
ANDREW MANSON - Veedal
PETER MANSON - Bloburn
JAMES MORRISON - Dykes
JESSIE MORRISON - Dykes
PETER PETERSON - Sloag
LILLIAN `Lilly` RATTER - Braidfit
MARGARET `Meggie` RATTER - Punds
WALTER RATTER - Punds
JEMIMA `Mima` ROBERTSON - Braidfit
WILLIE `Wullie` SMITH - Ham
ELIZABETH J. SMITH - Ham
JEANNIE THOMSON - Stoel
ANDREW UMPHRAY - Leraback
DAVID UPHPRAY - Mucklegrind
JAMES `Jimmy` UMPHRAY - Ristie
LOUISA `Liza` UMPHRAY - Brae
MARGARET `Maggie` UMPHRAY - Gravins
ROBERT `Robbie` UMPHRAY - North Harrier
ROBINA `Beenie`UMPHRAY - Lerabeck
SCOTTIE UMPHRAY - South Harrier
THOMAS UMPHRAY - Gravins
WILLIAM `Wullie` UMPHRAY - Ham

The Director
MICHAEL POWELL
1905 - 1990

Michael Latham Powell, son of Thomas and Mabel Powell, was the youngest of two sons and was born in Bekesbourne, Kent, England on 30th September 1905. His father, a hop farmer had moved to Kent from Worcestershire soon after his parents were married, and following a brief spell living at Howlett`s Farm, the family moved to a much larger place at Hoath Farm, Canterbury, a place which would inspire him greatly in later years into making a film there.

From here Michael attended King`s School and Dulwich College, where the First World War had brought about great changes in the Powell household, not least of all was the tragic loss of his elder brother John to appendicitis, closely followed by the death of his grandmother. Michael`s father during the war had been serving in the army in France, a place he had decided to settle when hostilities ceased. The farm had been run in his absence by a friend George Finn and his son Hugh, this eventually was sold and Michael and his mother joined his father in Marseilles, where he ran a hotel .

By 1922, his parents relationship having gone through turbulent times had ended in divorce and he found himself back in England and working as clerk at the National & Provincial Bank, an occupation with which he was not at all contented.

Around 1925 Michael, having left the bank, went back to France and his father introduced him to the Irish-born Hollywood movie director and producer Rex Ingram. Noted for his work on Rudolph Valentino`s *Four Horsemen of the Apocalypse* Rex had a studio in Nice and offered to take Michael on as an assistant, where he would do everything from make tea, carry equipment and act in bit parts, though at the same time keep a watchful eye on Mr Ingram and learn the ins and outs of the movie industry, Michael had always loved movies and marvelled at the work of great directors D.W.Griffith and Mr Ingram.

By 1927 Michael had worked on several low budget movies in a variety of roles, stills photographer, set designer, tile cutter, editor, camera operator and assistant director. His experience and passion for movie making, saw him return to London, where he worked his way up at Denham & Pinewood Studio`s to director status, producing short features known in the trade as `Quota Quickies` with a running time of an hour or thereabouts. The most notable being *Red Ensign* 1934.

In 1929 he got to work with that master of suspense, the late great Alfred Hitchcock as assistant cameraman on three of his movies *Champagne, The Manxman and Blackmail,* The latter was known for originally being filmed in silent and masterfully converted to sound. A year later Michael found himself working alongside Campbell Gullan as a writer and assistant director on the 70 minute movie *Caste* filmed at Walton Studio, Walton-on-Thames, Surrey. This would eventually lead to him directing 24 of his own movies between 1931 and 1936 including this all time classic *The Edge of the World* released in 1937.

Michael Powell went on to become one of Britain`s most iconic 20th century film directors, who in 1939 collaborated with Hungarian scriptwriter Emeric Pressburger to make a wartime thriller set around Scapa Flow, Orkney entitled *A Spy in Black,* produced by Alexander Korda. The movie was a great success and later the Powell & Pressburger partnership as the Archers Film Company continued to turn out such classics as *49th Parallel, One of Our Aircraft is Missing, The Life and Death of Colonel Blimp, A Canterbury Tale, I Know Where I`m Going, A Matter of Life and Death, Black Narcissus, The Red Shoes, Battle of the River Plate, and Gone to Earth* etc. All in all Michael was accredited to 60 movies as director, and 36 as a writer, ending with *`Return to the Edge of the World`* a BBC made for TV special on the making of his 1937 classic to act as bookends for the airing of the movie on TV.

Michael passed away on 19th February 1990 at his home in Avening, Gloucestershire after a long battle with cancer. He leaves two sons Columba and Kevin from his marriage to Frances Reidy (Died 5/7/83). Also his wife since 1984 and highly acclaimed Academy Award winning editor of Martin Scorsese` pictures, Thelma Schoonmaker .

THE MOVIE LOCATIONS THEN & NOW

In the opening scenes a yacht passes by the wedges of East Hoevdi, Foula
Photo: BFI & Estate of Michael Powell
Map key 01

East Hoevdi today minus the yacht. The giant rocks are easily recognisable
Photo: Author

Mr Graham`s yacht passes by the unique triple arch Gaada Stack in 1936
Photo: BFI & Estate of Michael Powell
Map key 02

One of Foula`s most famous landmarks the Gaada Stack some 70 years on
Photo: Author

Foula`s high sea cliffs seen in one of the opening sequences of the movie
Photo: BFI & Estate of Michael Powell
Map key 03

The cliffs at Westa Hoevdi seventy years on. The RMS *Oceanic* was wrecked near here on 8th September 1914.
Photo: Author

Mr & Mrs Graham (Michael Powell & Frankie Reidy) arrive at Ham Voe on Hirta
Photo: BFI & Estate of Michael Powell
Map key 04

Ham Voe 72 years on but with extended pier. Note where steps are in previous photo to the right of Frankie, and where the same steps appear here near the hand rail.
Photo: Author

Andrew Gray (Niall MacGinnis) at the abandoned croft of Gravins in Ham, Foula
Photo: BFI & Estate of Michael Powell

Gravins in 2008 was minus its roof, doors and windows but has now been bought for restoration by a couple of folk living on the island.
Photo: Author

Another shot of Andrew (Niall MacGinnis) at the abandoned croft at Gravins
Photo: BFI & Estate of Michael Powell
Map key 05

The croft of Gravins was used a number of times in the movie, including the Laird's visit and evacuation scenes. L to R: Sheila Gear, Donna Atherton, Author and Jeff Atherton
Photo: Geoff Bland

Andrew and the Graham`s arrive at the `Gone Over` stone at Da Nort Bank
Photo: BFI & Estate of Michael Powell
Map key 06

Looking along Da Nort Bank to where the `Gone Over` stone scene was filmed in 1936
Photo: Author

Bloburn at the north end of Foula was used as the Manson`s croft in the film
Photo: BFI & Estate of Michael Powell
Map key 07

At Bloburn in 2008, though the buildings are still there some changes were noted. The roof on the left has been re-tiled and the one on the right now has a tin roof.
Photo: Author

Local folk arrive at the Kirk for Sunday service with Hamnafield hill as a backdrop
Photo: BFI & Estate of Michael Powell
Map key 08

The auld Kirk at South Biggins, still retains its walls, but has no roof or windows and the north wall has been moved in line with the kirk after being damaged in a storm.
Photo: Author

The residents of Foula Inside the Kirk in 1936. (Names on p.74)
Photo: BFI & Estate of Michael Powell
Map key 08

Inside the auld Kirk as it stands today. The door space gives a sense of scale at 76.2 cm. How on Earth did Mr Powell get his crew and all those folk in here?
Photo: Author

A trio of actors Eric Berry, Belle Chrystall and Niall MacGinnis (Robbie,Ruth and Andrew) seen here at Smallie behind Da Noup.
Photo: BFI & Estate of Michael Powell

Behind Da Noup Close to the spot where Ruth,Andrew and Robbie were in 1936
Photo: Jennifer Ratter

The boat parliament meeting up at Da Ness, John (Hamish) is on the left. The top of the Gaada Stack can just be seen left of the man standing right.
Photo: BFI & Estate of Michael Powell

Map key 10

Sadly, wrong time of day for this photo. This is where the boat parliament took place at Da Ness in the far north of Foula. The big rock where Hamish stood is on the left.
Photo: Author

The women folk gather on the cliffs near Whirly Knowe to watch the climb
Photo: BFI & Estate of Michael Powell
Map key 11

Looking to South Ness from near to where the women-folk gathered for the climb

Photo: Dave Ramsey

John the Catechist (Hamish Sutherland) watches Andrew and Robbie climb the cliff from the auld Kirk window
Photo: BFI & Estate of Michael Powell

Inside the Kirk minus plaster, windows roof and altar, looking to the spot where John the Catechist stood watching the climb. Da Noup can be seen behind.
Photo: Author

James and Andrew Gray (Finlay Currie and Niall MacGinnis) at Bankwell Mill, with South Biggins, the old Kirk and Da Noup behind.
Photo: BFI & Estate of Michael Powell
Map key 11

What now remains of Bankwell Mill at Hame Banks on the southern tip of Foula
Photo: Author

Ruth and Peter Manson (Belle Chrystall and John Laurie) Head across Doon Banks or Da Wurrawusbanks south of the airstrip during the funeral bid scene
Photo: BFI & Estate of Michael Powell
Map key 13

Doon Banks to the south of Foula, where the funeral bid scene with Belle Chrystall and John Laurie was filmed
Photo: Author

Ruth (Belle Chrystall) sits by Mill Loch waiting for Andrew (Niall MacGinnis)
Photo: BFI & Estate of Michael Powell
Map key 14

Mill Loch with the large boulder on the right where Ruth (Belle Chrystall) sat waiting for her lover Andrew (Niall MacGinnis)
Photo: Author

James Gray (Finlay Currie) Discusses the poor harvest with John Isbister (Hamish Sutherland) at the Kail yard at South Biggins.
Photo: BFI & Estate of Michael Powell
Map key15

Owner of South Biggins Eric Isbister and visitor Geoff Bland at the old Kail yard. Mr Powell must have used a crane or scaffold for the camera as it was impossible to get the same angle as he did in 1936.

Photo: Authore

Peter Manson (John Laurie) spots the little mail boat sent out by Ruth and heads down off Soberlie towards the Gaada Stack at Da Ness.
Photo: BFI & Estate of Michael Powell
Map key 16

Following the route Peter Manson took in 1936 heading towards the Gaada Stack.
The Ristie croft, now holiday cottage can be seen on the far right of the photo.
Photo: Author

Ruth (Belle Chrystall) at Gaada Stack on Foula just after Peter finds the mail boat
Photo: BFI & Estate of Michael Powell
Map key 02

The Gaada stack is unique in having a triple arch.
Photo: Author

The old croft at Sloag with a tekkit roof as it was in 1936 during the scene of the Foula Reel dance sequence. Finlay Currie is walking the path with a lantern.
Photo: BFI & Estate of Michael Powell
Map Key 17

The sad ruins of the old croft at Sloag on the east side of the island, the track where Finlay walked is now all overgrown with green pasture.
Photo: Author

Andrew Gray (Niall MacGinnis) at Lerwick harbour, old buildings to the right are Lodberries, the most photographed houses in Lerwick.
Photo: BFI & Estate of Michael Powell

Map key 18

The author in the same spot at Lerwick, note that the crack in the harbour wall to the right of him can be seen in the previous photo, but with repairs evident
Photo: Author

Inside the derelict roofless croft at Veedal. This was used because it was perfect for light, all furniture and ornaments were put in to create the look of a dwelling
Photo: BFI & Estate of Michael Powell
Map key 19

The old croft at Veedal,Ham, still stands minus its roof ,though now missing the door and windows put in by the film crew to make it more authentic inside
Photo: Author

Peter Manson (John Laurie) at the end of the pier during the storm. Note how short pier is compared to the next photo with the new extension.
Photo: BFI & Estate of Michael Powell
Map key 04

Geoff Bland stands at the end of the newly extended pier. The large rock behind him can be made out in the previous photo with John Laurie
Photo: Author

The `Helliberg` rollers (See p.98) that Skeets Kelly filmed from a ledge of the cliff overhang, during the storm sequence in the movie.
Photo: BFI & Estate of Michael Powell

Map key 20

The ledge below the cliff overhang near Da skerry o Hellabrik
where cameraman Skeets filmed the crashing waves.
Photo: Author

KEY TO MOVIE LOCATIONS

1. East Hoevdi.	The Yacht Opening scene
2. Gaada Stack.	The Yacht & Ruth
3. Westa Hoevdi	Cliffs seen as yacht arrives
4. HamVoe.	Arrival & Evacuation etc
5. Gravins.	Andrew Arrival / Evacuation
6. Da Nort Bank.	Gone Over Stone
7. Bloburn.	Granny and Funeral
8. Kirk.	Sunday Service & Funeral
9. Smallie / Noup.	Robbie, Andrew, Ruth on hill
10. Da Ness.	Boat Parliament
11. Whirly Knowe.	Cliff climb spectators
12. Bankwell Mill.	Andrew in quern mill
13. Doon Bank.	Ruth and Peter funeral bid
14. Mill Loch.	Ruth sat on rock
15. Kailyard.	Poor Harvest South Biggins
16. Da Logat.	Peter after spotting mail boat
17. Sloag.	Foula Reel & Lullaby
18. Lerwick.	Andrew at the harbour
19. Veedal.	Ruth & Hamish in house
20. South Ness.	Storm ledge for Skeets

Note: It is suggested that anyone wishing to visit these locations, follow the country code and make enquiries with a Foula Heritage ranger first as a few are in dangerous locations.

Map courtesy Estate of Michael Powell

SHETLAND CHILDREN IN THE EDGE OF THE WORLD

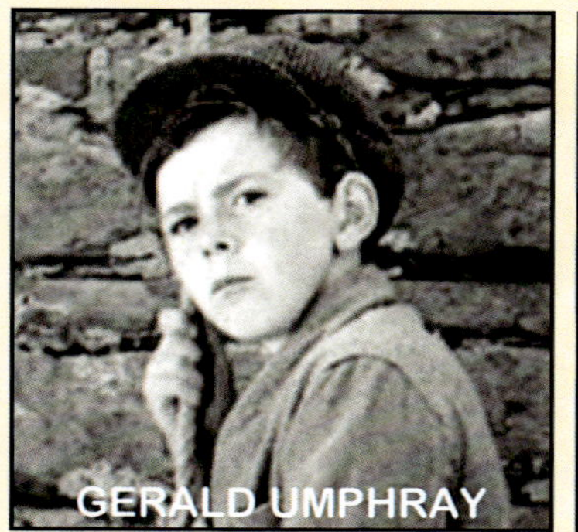
GERALD UMPHRAY

MARGARET GREIG

JESSAMINE SMITH

SOME KEY SCOTTISH PLAYERS IN THE MOVIE

CAMPBELL ROBSON

NIALL WITH GEORGE SUMMERS

JAMES GARRIOCK

FOULA FOLK IN THE EDGE OF THE WORLD

APPEARENCES OF LOCAL FOLK

The majority of Foula residents made an appearance at some point in `*The Edge of the World*` and here are some of those who were cast as extras and the parts they had to play.

Edith Gray
of Dykes

Edith now well into her 90s, was an attractive young girl of 18 in 1936 and remembers several sequences she was called to. Among them, the service in the Kirk, the gathering of the girls on the cliff for the climb, the caa and roo of the sheep near the Sneck, dancing in the Foula Reel, and waiving off Andrew at the pier when he left on the boat. I asked Edith who her favourite actor was? "*Mr MacGinnis was very nice, and a bit of a ladies man y`know*" she said with a smile. I then asked what other little things she remembered about the movie and she said " *I always remember there was a lot of waiting around, folk were told to go to a certain spot for a part in the film, and they would wait to have their name called then told what to do, we were paid sixpence when we got a part. Another time I remember being on the cliffs and the actress (Belle) throwing her binoculars to the ground after being told the man had fallen".* (It would seem this part ended up on the cutting room floor!). Edith, still with fond memories, has left Foula now and lives in a rest home on the mainland.

Maggie Henry
of North Harrier

Maggie had several scenes, the camera seemed to love her. In the Kirk she can be seen at the back next to Robbie Isbister. Then we see her again on the cliffs watching the climb with hand on hip and stern expression. Later in the movie as in the photo here we see her at the lullaby scene hand on jaw sat next to the elderly knitters Mrs Gray and Mrs Isbister. Maggie`s two daughters Bessie and Jessie also have parts in the Kirk service, a dance at the Foula Reel with James Andrew Gray and at the evacuation. It is believed she passed away in Scalloway on 17th July 1949.

Robbie Umphray of North Harrier had several scenes too, including the boat parliament, the lullaby scene, (Leaning in a doorway smoking his pipe, see photo p.76). Another appearance is when Andrew leaves the Isle and says goodbye, old Robbie gets to shake his hand. Sadly Robbie died the following year so never got to see the finished movie.

John Gray

John Gray Lived at Burns, a two story house and the largest croft on Foula, he was a real character and looked typical of what many of the St.Kilda folk looked like in the early 20th century, he was used for many a sequence, the boat parliament, the laird`s visit, Andrew leaving the isle where like Robbie Umphray he shakes the actors hand. His big scene was at the lullaby and Foula Reel where he is seen standing at a wall smoking his pipe, here he gets a big close up, and is loving every minute.

He later remarked about the Pier scene in Michael`s book: *`Maister Seabourne, I`m eighty years today. I`ve been a ride across the Isle in yon *car o`yours. I`ve had a close up taken by your camera and now I`m getting paid for standing on the jetty and smoking` me old pipe!`*. *The car imported by the film crew was the first on Foula and when the movie was finished it was sold to one of the Foula men.

Peter Peterson

Peter Peterson of Sloag, we don`t see too often in the movie as he is usually just one of the crowd, he first appears at the Kirk, where he gets a big close up, then later at the boat parliament. He is also among the men and women at the evacuation scene. Peter, like some of the other Foula folk had a second job with the film company, that of water carrier. In those days there were no plumbed in pipes so water was brought from Rossie`s loch in a large drum on a handcart and Peter and Wullie Umphray were given this task.

Jimmy Gray of Dykes also found employment as Camera Grip for Skeets Kelly. Jimmy appeared again at the reunion in the *Return to the Edge of the World* in 1978.

Robbie Isbister

Robbie Isbister a local merchant lived at South Biggins and we first see him inside the Kirk next to his make believe wife Maggie Henry, whom he gives a gentle nudge as she nods off during the sermon by John the Catechist (Hamish Sutherland). Robbie was chosen for a number of scenes and is seen outside the Kirk after the service stood next to Finlay Currie and John Laurie. Next we see him by the pier wall during the laird`s visit, then again at the scene where Andrew leaves for the mainland. He is also seen lighting up his pipe at the lullaby scene. Robbie in fact appeared in another film, that of a documentary made in 1956/57 entitled : Foula—The Edge of Britain. Robbie passed away at home on 25th November 1962.

34
36
37
30
35
33
32
26
31
19
13
29
27
28
25
24
23
20
21
14
15
16
17
18
8
9
12
11
10
4
5
6
7
1
2
3

FOULA FOLK IN THE KIRK 1936

1. JAMES `Jimmy` HENRY
2. LILLY RATTER (Nee Robertson)
3. WALTER RATTER
4. NIALL MACGINNIS (Actor)
5. BELLE CHRYSTALL (Actress)
6. ERIC BERRY (Actor)
7. JOHN LAURIE (Actor)
8. PETER PETERSON
9. JEMIMA `Mima`ROBERTSON
10. AGNES `Nannie`GRAY
11. JEANNIE THOMSON (Nee Gray)
12. UNKNOWN
13. JESSIE MORRISON (Nee Gray)
14. LOUISE `Louie` GRAY
15. EDITH GRAY
16. THOMAS `Tammie`GRAY
17. JEAN `Jeannie` GRAY (Nee Henry)
18. JAMES ANDREW GRAY
19. ANDREW MANSON
20. UNKNOWN
21. MARGARET `Maggie` RATTER
22. UNKNOWN.
23. POSS JEMIMA SMITH?
24. UNKNOWN.
25. JAMES `Jimmy`HENRY
26. UNKNOWN.
27. UNKNOWN.
28. ANDY GEAR
29. MARGARET `Maggie` HENRY
30. ROBERT `Robbie` ISBISTER
31. UNKNOWN.
32. ALFRED ISBISTER
33. JESSIE HENRY
34. ELIZABETH `Lizzie`ISBISTER
35. BESSIE HENRY
36. UNKNOWN (Poss Film crew?)
37. ELIZABETH J.SMITH

Kirk Photo & All named Foula folk photo`s : From `The Edge of the World` : BFI & Estate of Michael Powell.

AGGIE JEAN ISBISTER

Andy
Gear
Mima
Gear

PETER GRAY

SCOTTIE UMPHRAY

EDITH GRAY

DAVID UMPHRAY

THOMAS `Tammie` GRAY
ROBERT `Robbie` ISBISTER
PETER RATTER
ROBERT `Robbie` UMPHRAY
WILLIAM `Wullie` GEAR
JAMES `Jimmy` ISBISTER

JEMIMA ROBERTSON
GEORGE `Dodie` ISBISTER
PETER PETERSON
JAMES `Jimmy` HENRY
JOHN GRAY
PETER MANSON

CAST & CREW
BIOGRAPHIES

Peter Manson

John Laurie

1897 - 1980

John Paton Laurie who played Peter Manson in the movie was born in Dumfries, Scotland on 25th March 1897. The son of a mill worker, he attended local schools prior to taking a course in architecture at Dumfries Academy, which was cut short by him joining the army in the First World War. After the war, no longer wanting to pursue a career as an architect, he enrolled as a pupil in the Central School of Speech and Drama in London. Here he acted in his first stage play in 1921.

Described as a prolific Shakespearian actor, John was to appear in a number of plays at the Old Vic theatre in London and the Royal Shakespeare Theatre in Stratford-upon-Avon during the period 1922-1934 acting out roles in *Hamlet, Richard III* and *Macbeth.* He became acquainted with legendary British stage and screen actor Laurence Olivier, later appearing alongside him in four of his films, though prior to this he had been cast as a wages clerk in the 1934 movie *Red Ensign,* the story of a dockyard strike, directed by the great man himself Michael Powell.

Michael Powell had already decided from the very beginning that John would have a part in *The Edge of the World*, for apart from *Red Ensign,* he had already worked with Laurie on another of his movies *Her Last Affair* 1936 in which he played the part of Robb, the Innkeeper. But it was seeing John`s masterful display in the role of the crofter in Alfred Hitchcock`s *The 39 Steps* 1935 that convinced him. Though at the start Michael was not sure which character he would play. As we know with a little help from the make-up dept, his age went from 30 to 50 and he ended up as Peter Manson the father of Ruth and Robbie.

John`s role in *The Edge of the World* almost ended before it began, for prior to acting out his first scene with Kitty, Belle and Eric at Bloburn, he had been returning from a walk on Da Sneug (Highest hill on Foula at 1200ft) with Michael and John Seabourne, when negotiating a stone dyke on the way back, he jumped, his foot caught the wall and he crashed to the ground breaking his collar bone. The transport boat *Vedra* was in Scalloway so they had to use the mail boat to get him to hospital. It looked bad and they thought he would be out of the picture for months, but like a trouper he was back at work in four weeks, and John being the man he is, all he could do was curse himself for being an idiot.

John Laurie went on to make a further 142 appearances in both film and television, among them Michael Powell and Emeric Pressburger`s first colour movie *The Life and Death of Colonel Blimp* 1943, and another P&P movie *I Know Where I`m Going* 1945. John also met up with an old friend from Foula, Kitty Kirwan on the set of *Floodtide* 1949.

Other notable performances included parts in Walt Disney productions *Treasure Island* 1950 and *Kidnapped* 1960 but John is mostly remembered for his sterling role as Private Frazer in BBC TV sitcom *Dad`s Army*, appearing in 60 episodes from 1968-1977 with a movie spin off being made in 1971. It is interesting to note that of all the actors in the series about Britain`s soldiers of the Home Guard, John was the only one to have actually served in the Home Guard in the Second World War.

John was married to Oonah Veronica Todd-Naylor from 1928 until his passing on 23rd June 1980 at Chalfont St.Peter, Buckinghamshire.

James Gray

Finlay Currie

1878–1968

Born in Edinburgh, Scotland, on 20th January 1878, Finlay Jefferson Currie was one of the film industries best loved character actors, even though acting from the age of 20 on stage, it would be a further 32 years before he made his big screen debut appearing as Rennett in *The Old Man*, an Edgar Wallace mystery released in 1931.

Finlay married Maud Courtney in the late 1890s and they had three Children. The couple had met during a song and dance act in New York. He was to appear in various supporting roles in some 20 movies prior to working with Mr Powell on *The Edge of the World* as veteran fisherman James Gray.

At the time of the screen tests for the actors in the island film, all but James Gray had been cast. Michael was beginning to get worried when a call from the agent Picot sent him dashing to the office, where he found Finlay sitting in the biggest chair in the place, and he was, as Michael said in his autobiography: *`Beaming all over, in grey tweeds, grey hair and glorious suede shoes. `Finlay!` I cried, Is this true? Would you play the part? It doesn`t carry anything like your money you know`.*

He waived his hand in a lordly manner. `I hate the stuff, chief`, he said. It`s the wonderful summer and the wonderful part in a fine film that I`m after. If I can bring Maud, I`m your man`. `Maud?` `My wife. Don`t worry. I know there`s no room on the island. She will stay in Lerwick for the present time and she will love it as much as I did., for you know Michael, I have been to Foula`. `You haven`t!`. `Aha, that shook you! Thirty years ago in a wee boat. So you see, it`s fated. Well?` `It`s a deal: and Finlay, I`m tickled to death to have you. I never dreamed you would be able to get away.

`Do you think I would miss a trip like this?. Besides this is the third picture where we`ve nearly worked together. We have got to break the spell. When do we leave?`. `The day after tomorrow`.

Like other members of the cast and crew, Finlay worked with Michael again on the *49th Parallel* 1941 and *I Know Where I`m Going* 1945, in the former of which was his old Foula friend Niall MacGinnis. Finlay also found himself working alongside other *Edge of the World* cast members from time to time, Belle Chrystall for one in *Follow Your Star* 1938 and John Laurie met him again in *Treasure Island* in 1950.

All in all, Finlay appeared in 140 roles in both movies and TV over the years. He performed in such classics as *Bonnie Prince Charlie* 1948, *Quo Vadis* 1951, *Ivanhoe* 1952, *Around the World in 80 Days* 1956, *The Fall of the Roman Empire* 1964 and his last movie *Bunny Lake is Miss*ing 1965. Memorable TV appearances include *Danger Man, Gideon`s Way, Prisoner and The Saint.*

Finlay who left us some of the most memorable moments in movie history, passed away on 9th May 1968 at Gerrards Cross, Buckinghamshire, England aged 90.

Andrew Gray

Niall MacGinnis

1913–1977

Born in Dublin, Ireland on 29th March 1913, Patrick Niall MacGinnis was educated at Stoneyhurst College, Clitheroe, Lancashire and Trinity College (The University of Dublin) where he studied medicine. He also attended drama school and took to stage acting during the 1930s. A switch from stage to screen came in 1935 when Niall was cast as John Lunn in *The Turn of the Tide* with John Garrick. Next came the role of Lieutenant Peter Stretton in *Dept of Honour* 1936.

Michael had heard of MacGinnis and seen his performance in *Turn of the Tide*, he thought that perhaps he would be good for the part of Andrew and sought out his agent Wilfred J.(Bill) O`Bryan to see if he was available for *The Edge of the World.* On arrival at his office, Bill said he had big plans for Niall, but when he heard about the part he would be playing, he sent Niall along to meet him, and as soon as they met Michael decided there and then that he was just right for the part.

Niall proved perfect for the role of Andrew Gray and like other members of the cast he went on to work with Michael and Emeric Pressburger in the *49th Parallel* 1941, playing the part of a German U-Boat sailor named Vogel, a part which almost got him arrested a short while after the movie was finished.

The incident happened while returning to Holyhead, Anglesey, North Wales from Ireland during the Second World War, MacGinnis was stopped by police and searched. They found a photo in his wallet showing him in a German uniform standing next to a U-boat and immediately thought they had captured a German spy. Niall was arrested and spent some time in a cell at the local police station, until documents were eventually provided to prove his innocence and that the picture had been taken on the set while he was acting in the movie.

As well as his acting career, he eventually qualified as a house surgeon and during the Second World War he had served in the Royal Navy in this post. Nevertheless he continued to act in a number of movies such as *The Day Will Dawn* 1942, *We Dive at Dawn* 1943, *Undercover* 1944, *Tawny Pipet* 1944 and *Henry V* 1944.

Niall was a splendid character actor and was often barely recognisable from his appearance as Andrew Gray. During the 1950s he starred alongside many of the Hollywood greats in such epics as : *Martin Luther* 1953, *Hell Below Zero* 1954, *Knights of the Round Table* 1954, *Helen of Troy* and *Alexander the Great* and *Lust for Life* all 1956, Then came *The Night of the Demon* 1957 and the *Nuns Story* 1959. In the 1960 he was alongside his old pal from Foula, John Laurie in Walt Disney`s *Kidnapped.*

He also played a most memorable role as Zeus in *Jason and the Argonauts* 1963. Others include *The War Lord* and *The Spy Who Came in From the Cold* both 1965 and *Shoes of a Fisherman* 1968.

In his last movie before retiring from acting in 1973 he was given a small part as Warder in *The Mackintosh Man* with Hollywood legend Paul Newman. In 1974 Niall, a qualified physician returned to medicine and practiced in both his native Ireland at Ballycullen, Ashford, Co Wicklow and at Haverfordwest, Pemrokeshire, a place where he lived with his wife Sheila and daughter Eleonore. Sadly he died of cancer in Newport, Dyfed, Wales on 6th January 1977,and even more tragically his 22 year old daughter died that same year.

Ruth Manson

Belle Chrystall

1910 - 2003

Belle by name and Belle by nature, this glamorous English actress was born in Preston, Lancashire on 25th April 1910, she was the daughter of Mr & Mrs Edward Chrystall of Preston, and attended Preston School for Girls, Westbourne High School and Cheltenham Ladies College and wishing to pursue a career in acting applied and was accepted at the Royal Academy of Dramatic Arts in 1927, where one of her fellow students was none other than Charles Laughton.

Her first appearance came in 1928 in a stage play entitled `*Crime*` and a few other small production roles were to follow, but Belle wanted to get into movies and auditioned for the part of Peggy in romantic comedy, a Michael Balcon production *A Warm Corner* 1930, which she got. A year later she was cast alongside James Harcourt in the movie *Hobson`s Choice* playing Vicky Hobson. Then came *Hindle Wakes* 1931 with Edmund Gwenn and Sybil Thorndyke, where Belle gave a sterling performance as mill worker Jenny Hawthorne.

A big break came in 1934 when she co-starred with Stewart Rome as Mavis Tremayne in *The Girl in the Flat*. The following year she had top billing in *Key to Harmony*. But it was her role in *Hindle Wakes* that had caught the attention of Michael Powell and as soon as her agent said she was available, Michael knew he had his Ruth Manson for *The Edge of the World.*

Belle travelled up to Shetland by plane with some of the cast and crew and was to spend the whole five months in accommodation at the Haa (Hall) on Foula with Frankie Reidy, Michael Powell`s future wife. Fortunately the pair got on well together and often gave the boys a run for their money when it came to laying down rules and regulations at Rock City.

Michael said of her in his book: *`When I saw Belle I could have kicked myself for wasting so much time. I knew what a good actress she was and in looks she was ideal. A fine young face, with deep eyes and broad forehead, the hair sweeping naturally off it, a sensitive mouth, a head set cleanly on good shoulders and a strong supple figure. Everyone knows how splendid she was in Hindle Wakes and I had also made a cast of her for a part at Warner`s, which she only failed to get because of the very strength and confidence which made her ideal for Ruth `.*

Though having much success with her role in *The Edge of the World*, with *Follow Your Star* 1938 a musical co-starring with Arthur Tracy, her role as Mary did not have the same impact, though she did manage to command major parts in several other movies of the late 1930s, *Yellow Sands* 1938, *Anything to Declare* 1938, *Breakers Ahead* 1938 and *Poison Pen* 1939, nothing came close to her performances in *Hindle Wakes* and *The Edge of the World.*

Belle`s final appearance on silver screen came in 1940 in *The House of the Arrow,* a murder mystery in which she played Ann Upcott, co-starring with Kenneth Kent and Diana Churchill. A few plays for the BBC then followed, and a brief modelling spell as the face of Lux soap. But by 1946 she had announced her retirement and settled down to family life with her husband Roy Proctor and baby daughter Chrystal. born in 1947.

Michael Powell returned to Foula in 1978 to make the BBC short documentary *Return to the Edge of the World*. Belle was asked if she would accompany him and others of the cast and crew, but she politely refused, saying that she much preferred to leave her 1930s image back in the day. She passed away in England on 7th June 2003.

Robbie Manson

Eric Berry

1913 - 1993

Eric Berry, son to Frederick William Berry and Louisa Danielson, was born in London on 9th January 1913. He attended City of London School and enrolled as an apprentice for stage acting at the Royal Academy of Dramatic Art in the late 1920s. In April 1931 Eric made his first stage appearance in the Everyman Theatre production of *Spilt Milk* at Hemel Hampstead and the following year made his West End Theatre debut in *The Cathedral.*

Never having acted in movies before *The Edge of the World* would be his golden opportunity to change all that. He was discovered by Chris Mann who was assigned by casting agent Picot Schooling to find suitable applicants for the various roles in the film and when Michael first met him this was his impression: *`He was tall and dark and his eyes were intolerant. He was not quite tough enough for an islander, but he was an actor, that was evident. It was important that Robbie should have charm and intelligence and Berry had both. I could not quite make up my mind about him. I decided this was because I had not yet found Andrew`.*

Michael needn`t have worried, for Eric it turns out was perfect for the part, and agile enough to be able to run the hills and climb the cliffs for the race with Andrew, and being single would not mind being away from home for five long months during production. In his autobiography Michael remarked: *`He was short-sighted and could do nothing without his glasses. He was only conscious of a void full of noises, wheeling seabirds, and the thunder of Atlantic rollers on the rocks 600ft below him. It was just as well. We all took chances...... I had Eric sprawled on the tip of a waterfall where Hoevdi Burn plunges over the cliff into the sea, where boats looked as small as toys far below. It occurred to me that I might be taking advantage of his amiable nature, and I sent Hamish and Syd Streeter down with ropes onto the ledge below to catch him when he fell. The sequence finished. Eric changed his wet clothes, asked for his glasses and trudged back to base to resume reading his book`.*

Following *The Edge of the World*, Eric had a minor part in Powell & Pressburger`s *Contraband* 1940, and as Dmitri in *The Red Shoes* 1948. Throughout the 1950s and 60s he played roles in various TV series, *The Adventures of Sea Hawk* 1958, *Omnibus* 1960, *Vanity Fair* 1961, *The Man from Uncle* 1964 .

Eric eventually returned to theatre and starred as Charles in the hit musical *Pippin* at the Imperial Theatre, Broadway in Mid-town Manhattan, New York. The show ran from 23rd October 1972 until 12th June 1977, and achieved a record total of 1,944 performances.

While living in America he was married briefly to English-born American film and musical theatre actress Constance Carpenter, whom it believed he had met on the set of the Broadway production of *The King and I* in 1952. During the Second World War Constance had entertained the troops in Europe, Asia and the Middle East, and on returning to the United States in 1950, she took American citizenship.

In 1977 following the successful theatre run of *Pippin*, Eric returned to TV acting and was cast in the role of Ambassador Kaiwi in the American TV crime drama *The Andros Targets* in an episode entitled *The Smut Peddler*. His last role was playing alongside Louis Gossett Jr as Rashad in the movie *Sadat* 1983, A dramatization of the life of Egyptian leader Muhammad Anwar al-Sadat, from his early years as a young officer fighting the British to his assassination in 1981. Retirement took Eric to Laguna Beach in a California, where sadly after a battle with cancer, Eric passed away on 2nd September 1993.

John the Catechist

Grant Sutherland

Grant Sutherland was a six foot something giant of a man, with thick set jaw and stern but dashing appearance. He hailed from Edinburgh and was cast as one of the key actors in *The Edge of the World* playing the part of John Isbister - The Catechist. He had acted on stage in Edinburgh with the Ad Astra theatre group but this was his first movie.

Known to all as Hamish, very little is known of his early background but following on from this movie made in 1936, he appeared in just five other movies, *Breakers Ahead* 1938, alongside Belle Chrystall who was the star of the movie. The Powell & Pressburger movie *The Spy in Black* 1939,in which he played Special Constable Bob Bratt. *What Men Live By* 1939, *The Proud Valley* 1940 and *Nine Men* 1941.

Hamish joined the army in 1941 and served actively overseas. He became a businessman in the world of finance after the war rather than go back into acting. Though he did make one final appearance on film in 1978, when along with his wife Joan he joined Michael Powell, John Laurie and Sydney Streeter on Foula for a short BBC documentary on the making of the 1936 movie entitled *Return to the Edge of the World*.

Jean Manson

Kitty Kirwan

1857 - 1950

Irish actress Kitty Kirwan was perhaps better known in Ireland for her performances on stage rather than film. Though she is known to have appeared in at least seven movies other than *The Edge of the World* 1936 in which she portrayed the Grandmother *Jean Manson.* These were *Macushla* 1937, *The Vicar of Bray* 1937, *The Londonderry Air* 1938, *Who Goes Next* 1938, *I Know Where I`m Going* 1945 the latter of which she once again teamed up with Michael Powell and crew for this movie made on the Isle of Mull and *Odd Man Out* 1947

Her last movie for the production company Aquila was *Floodtide* 1949 where she played the small role of Granny Shields, starred Gordon Jackson and her old Foula film companion John Laurie.

In his book *200,000 Feet on Foula*, Michael described Kitty`s journey up to Foula: *"Kitty was sent for by cable as soon as we fixed our schedule. She was told to hurry"*. And hurry she did! *"She caught the night express, grabbed a plane at Aberdeen, raced across Shetland by car, took a flying jump on the waiting Vedra, and arrived at Rock City* (Foula film huts) *in twenty seven hours. Not bad for an eighty year old"*.

Producer

Joe Rock

1893 - 1984

Joe Rock, born on Christmas day 1893 in New York City, New York, was an actor, producer and assistant director on over 120 movies from 1919—1955. Joe, a former Vaudeville comedian, began his film career as a silent actor in comedy shorts soon after leaving the army when the First World War ended, but became more and more interested in the business side of things. He became producer on around a dozen two-reel shorts starring Laurel & Hardy and also produced Michael Powell`s first feature for Joe Rock Studio *The Man Behind The Mask* in 1936.

When Michael first approached Joe with the idea for the movie about St.Kilda, being made on that island, Joe was full of enthusiasm, and backed the film 100%. But was in doubt when the island became unavailable and they had to move to the Shetland Isles. He went through some worrying times when problems with the weather, the camera crew and other snags started to occur, but in the end, it all worked out and MP delivered the goods.

Joe was married to Australian stage and screen actress Louise Granville until her death on 28th December 1968. They had two children. Joe passed away on 5th December 1984 at his home in Sherman Oaks, California. USA.

Cyril Ray - *Musical Director* 1908 - 1991

Born in Chorlton, Manchester on 16th March 1908, Cyril was known more for his work in later life as a radio commentator and journalist than his early musical attributes. However, aside from his work on the music for *The Edge of the World*, he had worked on the scores for several movies previous : *A Royal Romance* 1930, *Strictly Legal* 1935, *One Good Turn* 1936, *Excuse My Glove* 1936, *Everything is Rhythm* 1936, *The Man Behind The Mask* 1936, *Captain Bill* 1936, *Sing As You Swing* 1937 and Cotton Queen also 1937.

Sir Hugh S. Robertson - *Conductor* 1874 - 1952

Born in Glasgow on 23rd February 1874, Hugh was a musician, Scottish composer and founder of the Glasgow Orpheus Choir (formally the Toynbee Musical Association) in 1906. According to legend he was a perfectionist, he expected the highest standards of performance from all choir members. Its voice was a choir voice, and individual voices were not to be tolerated. Their repertoire included many Scottish folk songs arranged for choral performance, and for this reason the choir was chosen for *The Edge of the World*, where three songs would be used, the title, the lullaby and a lament at the funeral. The choir was also employed on *I Know Where I`m Going* 1945. Hugh Robertson died 7th October 1952.

W. Lambert Williamson - *Orchestrator* 1907 - 1975

Lambert was born in Cleethorpes, Lincolnshire on 28th April 1907. During his musical career spanning four decades he was musical director/conductor on thirty nine movies, a composer for twenty six other films, and provided the soundtrack for a further nine other movies. One of those twenty six was *The Edge of the World* . He also worked with Michael again on *A Matter of Life and Death* 1946. Other credits include : *Beat the Devil* 1952, *Romeo & Juliet* 1954, *Heaven Knows Mr Alison* 1956 and *Look Back in Anger* 1959. Lambert retired to Chiltern, Beaconsfield, Buckinghamshire, where he died on 13th November 1975.

Gerald Blattner - *Production Manager* 1913 -?

Born in Liverpool in 1913 but the family moved when he was just an infant and Gerry as he was known grew up in Hertfordshire. His father was Ludwig Blattner, film producer and inventor, and owned Blattner Studio`s in London. Gerry followed in his father`s footsteps and was production supervisor for the film *My Lucky Star* 1933. He and his first wife Pamela later lived in Elstree while working for Warner Bros, next door to Simon Cowell`s parents and Gerry according to Cowell`s unauthorized biography by Chas Newkey-Burden, is credited with helping Simon get into show business.

Gerry was production manager on *The Edge of the World* and was based at Elstree (Former Blattner) Studio in London.. He is perhaps best known for producing the 1960 movie *The Sundowners* starring Robert Mitchum and Debra Kerr.

Production Staff

Vernon A. Sewell

1903 - 2001

Vernon Campbell Sewell was born in London, England on 4th July 1903. He was educated at Marlborough College. Like John Seabourne, Michael had met Vernon at Nettlefold Studios, Surrey while working on the editing for one of his movies. Vernon was in the sound department at that time but could improvise and turn his hand to anything.

Very little has been written about Vernon, who was a sound engineer, writer, producer and director among other things in a film career spanning almost 40 years. Michael describes him as only he could: *`Vernon got his job at the studio through nepotism, but he retained it by sheer competence. He is the most competent man I have ever known. When consulted about an estimate for anything from a model of Big Ben to the interior of a submarine, Vernon snorts `Ridiculous! Daylight robbery`, tears up the estimate and does the job himself. His hobby is boats—From steam or diesel to outboard. But he never keeps a boat long, he does it up....then sells it and buys another one`.*

Needless to say Vernon ended up as Skipper on *The Edge of the World* film crew steam yacht *Vedra.*

Apart from the movie *The Silver Fleet* 1943 Written and Directed by Vernon under the guidance of Michael Powell for the Archers, he had a break from the industry when he joined the Navy, and was given command of a Coastal Defence Vessel which would operate from the Isle of Wight. Then, with the war over he was back on form as a director working on two pictures in 1945, *The World Owes Me a Living* and *Latin Quarter.* He directed another twenty four movies up to 1963 when he was asked to work on five episodes of a TV series *The Human Jungle* starring Herbert Lom. His movies include : *The Black Widow* 1951, *Ghost Ship* 1952, *Where There`s a Will* 1954, *Home and Away* 1956, *Rogue`s Yarn* 1957, *House of Mystery* 1961 and *Strictly for the Birds* 1963.

Following some work on a TV series, he was back to movies and directed a couple of horror flicks in 1968, *The Blood Beast Terror* and *Curse of the Crimson Altar.* An episode of the TV hit *The Avengers* followed in 1969, then his last movie *Burke and Hare* 1972 prior to his retirement. Vernon passed away in Durban, South Africa on 21st June 2001.

William H. Farr - *Production Staff.*

Little is known of Mr Farr, only that he was a close friend of Vernon Sewell (Skipper of the crew boat *Vedra*). He was part of the production team for *The Edge of the World* and is mentioned on a few occasions in Michael`s autobiography thus: *`The camera crew were already ahead of us, in Lerwick with the cameras. John and Syd, with the base camp nearly completed were on Foula. With them was Buddy Farr, a staunch friend of Vernon`s and a Jack-of-all-trades`.*

It would seem that Buddy as he was known, also attended the reconnaissance trip to Orkney with Michael, Vernon and Bill Paton for *A Spy in Black* 1939 starring Conrad Veidt . Buddy was also Assistant Director on *What Men Live By 1939,* with one of the cast being Grant Sutherland.

William Jamieson Paton - *Production Staff.* 1914 - 1997

Born in Lerwick, Shetland on 14th October 1907, son of Arthur James and Charlotte Jane Paton. He was known as Bill Paton throughout his three decades of working with Michael Powell and Emeric Pressburger on twelve of their movies. His job on Foula sounded less glamorous than most, but was one of the most important on set, that of unit caterer. Bill worked under Mrs Rutherford, the film crew`s housekeeper and together with a small contingent of the local populace who had been employed by the company, had to source, prepare and provide all the meals for the film unit. A mammoth task!. Also, aside from the catering, he was recruited as an extra for the Foula reel, a dance sequence in the movie.

Largely unaccredited in Michael`s movies, Bill was Michael`s personal assistant and a good friend, who would join him on most of his movie expeditions. Once an aspiring young footballer, he had intended to play professional but a knee injury soon ended that dream. Instead he went into the bakery and confectionary business prior to being spotted by Powell and recruited for *The Edge of the World`*. Bill finally got credited in *Peeping Tom* 1960. The pair stayed friends for years and no doubt shared many fond memories of hiking trips in the mountains of the Scottish Highlands, a place they both loved to escape to. Bill, who had married Myrtle Horton in the summer of 1945, Sadly passed away on 29th September 1997 in the hospital at Canterbury.

Production Staff
Sydney S. Streeter
1910 - 1989

A master carpenter, production manager, producer and later assistant director on movies spanning five decades, Sydney Stanley Stephen Streeter, known simply as Syd, was born in Falmouth, Cornwall on 10th December 1910 (BDM has 1911) He was in the RAF during the war and became a Pilot Officer in Aug 1945. He married Ivy M. Hood at Hendon in the summer of 1940 and they had one daughter.

Syd was one of the first to arrive on Foula and was daubed Chief of Construction. He was in charge of building all the accommodation huts for the cast and crew which would be sited behind the Haa. Aside from the huts he had to construct a railway track for the camera at Sloag, remove the roof from the Kirk to allow light in, then replace it again for other shots, plus build bridges and gangplanks for the evacuation scene. A very busy man.

He worked on many others as Producer/Assistant director, including Powell & Pressburger films : *49th Parallel, The Red Shoes, Gone to Earth and Battle of the River Plate*. He also produced *Return to the Edge of the World* . He died in Harrow, Middlesex in Dec 1989.

Bill Sweeny - *Recording Engineer* 1903 -

William Hubert Oliver Sweeny was the eldest of four children born in Ulverston, Cumbria in 1903. Bill Sweeny who was the Sound Recordist on Michael Powell`s *The Edge of the World* in `1937, was the RAF FPU's (Film Production Unit) sound recording expert, having also worked in the feature industry before the war. He had been put in charge of acquiring the FPU's sound equipment when it was formed and was subsequently responsible for some pioneering recordings, a famous one being of a crew's intercom commentary during a bomber operation entitled *Operational Height* and Like most of the FPU's subsequent productions, a cast consisting of Service personnel was used. The shooting of movie began on 25 March 1942 and finished on 4 June. The completed film, which ran to four reels, was shown to the Air Council on 15 November that same year .

Between 1935 and 1956 Bill, who was usually credited as W.H.O. Sweeny, had worked on a total of 14 movies,

Lionel K.Tregellas - *Sound Engineer* 1904 - 1976

Often credited as L.K.Tregellas, his full name was Lionel Keith Anthony Tregellas, but known affectionately as `*The Puffin*` to Michael Powell and his band of merry men on Foula. He was the sound engineer for *The Edge of the World.* He had great responsibility for all aspects of making sure recordings projected with clarity, and with the howling winds, screeching birds and crashing waves on Foula, he certainly had his work cut out.

In fact Thelma Schoonmaker once recalled with great mirth a remark made in Michael`s book about a telegram he received after sending the daily rushes back to the studio, it read: *`Viewed your rushes, sound inaudible, picture invisible, is this intentional?`* Which gives some idea of the trouble these poor technicians had to endure. Lionel who worked in the sound department for BBC TV News in later life, retired in the early 1970s and lived in Truro, Cornwall. He died on 23rd February 1976.

John Arthur Seabourne - *Editor* 1890 - 1960s

John, credited as A. Seabourne in *The Edge of the World*, was for a time Michael Powell`s editor and right hand man and second unit director on the set of this movie, though a cruel twist of fate was to intervene and he never saw the picture through. Due to rupture of duodenal ulcers and a severe haemorrhage, he had to be put on the *Vedra* film crew boat and sent to the mainland where he was hospitalized and had to convalesce for quite some time afterwards. Fortunately editor Derek Twist stepped in to save the film and John eventually recovered, but he was by no means cured.

Michael had met John at a Nettlefold Studio, Walton-on-Thames, Surrey in 1931 where he had arrived to make his first feature film *Two Crowded Hours*, John would work as editor for this and all his other movies up to and including *I Know Where I`m Going.* 1941 with spells out for illness during the Foula film and in 1940 and 41.

John lived with his wife Margaret and two sons, both of whom were in the film industry. He had been born in Colchester, Essex in 1890. Though the date is not certain he is understood to have passed away in the mid-1960s.

Editor
Derek Twist
1905 - 1979

Derek N.Twist was born in London, England on 26th May 1905. He is known as a writer, editor, producer, director and in fact actor in on at least one occasion. Though his ability as an editor was second to none, and Michael Powell recalled how he saved the day with `*The Edge of the World*` when current editor John Seabourne fell ill and once remarked "He had the eye of a hawk, the memory of an Indian and a heart of granite" .

Prior to the Foula film Derek had worked with Alfred Hitchcock and edited *The 39 Steps* in 1935.and in fact he was called back for both the 1959 and 1978 versions. Other notable works include : *They Drive by Night* 1938, *The Lion Has Wings* 1939, *Green Grow The Rushes* 1951 and in 1952 he wrote the screenplay and produced *Angels One Five* which starred Jack Hawkins and John Gregson.

In 1945 while working on the movie *Journey Together* with Richard Attenborough, Jack Watling and David Tomlinsion, he even got a small role as a Wing Commander on an aircrew selection board. Following retirement, Derek lived with wife Nessie in Chelmsford, where sadly he passed away at home on 15th August 1979.

Ernest Palmer *Camera* 1901- 1964

Born Harold Ernest Palmer in St. Pancras, London, England in 1901, Ernie was a British cinematographer, sometimes credited as H.E. Palmer. He worked at Elstree Studio in the 1930's and at Ealing in the early 1940's and was camera operator on two of Michael`s pictures, *The Man Behind The Mask* 1936 and *The Edge of the World*, taking over from Monty Berman.

He later worked feature films such as *Chamber of Horrors* 1940, *The Ghosts of Berkley Square* 1947 and in the TV series *The Adventures of Sir Lancelot* 1956-57 (21 episodes) and *The Adventures of Robin Hood* 1957 (6 episodes) He died at home in West Ealing, London Middlesex aged 63 on 12 March 1964.

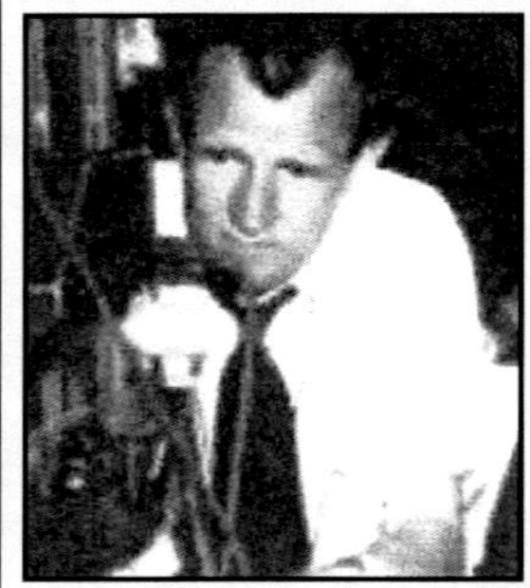

Camera

Skeets Kelly

1913 - 1970

Born in Newcastle-upon-Tyne on 10th November 1913. Skeets Who`s real name was Graham White Kelly, grew up in Co.Wicklow, Ireland. White incidentally stems from his mother`s maiden name and Skeets was a nickname he had acquired prior to joining the Foula film crew.

The Edge of the World was to be the first movie Skeets worked on with Michael Powell and was described by Michael to have been one of his *'Foula Regulars'* and thus *'Worth three other men'*. One of the best cinematographers in the business, Skeets often risked life and limb to get the shots wanted and during the Foula film was often seen scrambling down cliffs to film dramatic sequences. One such occasion was remembered by Michael in his book `200,000 Feet on Foula` : *`We never tired of watching the Helliberg rollers. I spent hours scrambling near the surf until I found places where the waves could almost break over the camera without danger. Then I would reappear on ground level and soon another wave-shot for the storm sequence was in the bag. I found one horrifying place where the rock made a perfect breakwater to a deep, round geo. Underneath the overhang was a shelf. It was possible to get down there and be inside the wave as it shot overhead and dropped like the sky into a boiling geo. Only danger was that the backwash of a big wave would sweep the climber off. This did not deter Skeets who spent a happy half hour down there with his camera`*. He later worked with Michael again on the *49th Parallel* 1941.

During the war Skeets served with the RAF FPU (Film Production Unit) Filming bomber operations for wartime propaganda movies and training films. His camera work on *Operational Height* was described as being of an innovative quality. Skeets had already flown twenty four missions and was recommended for the DFC when he was shot down over France. It was 27th August 1943. The target was to be Gosnay power station SW of Bethune, and Skeets, a Flying Officer on loan from 88 Squadron was detailed to film the raid. However, his aircraft Boston BZ237 of 107 Sqdn was first hit by flak which damaged one of its two engines. The aircraft was then pounced on by an Fw 190 and the pilot F/O J.C.Allison was forced to make a crash landing in a field about ten miles south of St.Omer. Fortunately all the crew including Skeets survived, and for a couple of months evaded capture, but eventually were caught by the Gestapo and spent the rest of the war in a PoW camp. NB: For further info on the latter raid see `RAF Evaders` by Oliver Clutton-Brock. ISBN 978-0753722794.

After the war Skeets returned to the movie industry and is credited with work on over 56 pictures including: *Great Expectations* 1946, *Treasure Island* 1950 (With John Laurie once again) *Ivanhoe* 1952 (With Finlay Currie again) *Around the World in 80 Days* 1956, *A Night to Remember* 1958, *The Sundowners* 1960, *The War Lover* 1962, *Lawrence of Arabia* 1962, *Lord Jim* 1965, *The Blue Max* 1966 and *The Battle of Britain* 1969.

In August 1970, Skeets had just finished work on Alistair MacLean`s *Puppet on a Chain* and was in Dublin, Ireland working on *When Eight Bells Toll* when the production office working on the movie *Zeppelin* with Michael York, asked if he could be loaned for a weekend to do some aerial shots for the movie.

On 18th August Skeets was in camera helicopter Alouette G-AWEE filming the aerial sequences of the biplanes making their attack on an airship near Baldonnel, when one of the aircraft, an SE.5A replica EI-ARB collided in mid-air with the helicopter at 2,000 feet, the pair fell into Irish Sea. The Irish Air Corp pilot Jim Liddy in the SE.5A and sadly all on board the Alouette, pilot Gilbert Chomat "Gilly", camera man Skeets Kelly and director Burch Williams were killed.

Monty Berman - *Camera* 1912 - 2006

Born Nestor Montague Berman in Whitechapel, London, Monty as he was known was educated at University College, Hampstead On graduation he worked for Twickenham Studios and became a cameraman later working with Ernest Palmer. He was given a chance to work with Michael on *The Edge of the World,* but was plagued with technical problems and only filmed a few scenes before being replaced by Ernie. His later career really took off as a producer in television and he is best known for *The Saint, The Champions, Randell & Hopkirk, Department S* and *Jason King* in the 1960s and *The Adventurer* in 1970s. Monty died on aged 93 on 20th June 2006.

George Black Jr - *Assistant Production Manager* 1911 -

Born in Sunderland the son of George and Hannah Black, George was loaned by Gerry Blattner to assist on Foula with anything that might be needed. He dealt with ordering materials, supplies and general liaison. Once work on *The Edge of the World* was finished, he wrote, produced and co-produced a few movies i.e. *Trouble in the Air* 1948, *The Perfect Woman* 1949, but ended up going in business with his brother Alfred running Black Brothers TV Ltd.

SAILING VESSELS USED IN THE MOVIE

Throughout the film various marine craft from rowing boats to Steamships were used, though nobody had ever really taken note of the types, registration numbers or names of these before. With many Shetlanders having a keen interest in maritime history and pre-war fishing fleets, I thought I would take this opportunity to list some of the many boats that were seen in the film that I was able to identify.

The movie itself begins with Niall MacGinnis, Michael Powell, and Frankie Reidy who are aboard a white Yacht belonging to Island owner Alistair Holbourn as they navigate their way around Foula.

Above left: Frankie Reidy and Michael Powell aka Mr & Mrs Graham arrive at the pier at Ham Voe, Foula. Their Yacht can be seen in the background and the tender in the photo on the right.

Photo: BFI & Estate of Michael Powell.

Other vessels seen are the tender used with the yacht and the Fourerns used by John Laurie, Finlay and Shetlanders during the cliff climb sequence, these were 4 oar clinker built rowing boats and four were used during filming at the Knab, Lerwick. Also the Steam Yacht *Vedra* used by the film crew as a supply vessel to ferry food, equipment and building materials over from Scalloway.

The *Vedra* also appeared in a couple of scenes in the movie. First where the Laird visited the isle, then during the evacuation of the islanders and their possessions and livestock.

The boats used for the cliff climb on Foula. This sequence was the last to be filmed and the boats were shot below the Knab, Lerwick on the Shetland Mainland.

Photo: BFI & Estate of Michael Powell

The crew supply vessel the S.Y. `Vedra` seen here at anchor alongside the pier on Foula.

Photo: BFI & Estate of Michael Powell

When Andrew Gray (Niall MacGinnis leaves `Hirta` (Foula) for the Mainland, he is seen in Lerwick harbour where he seeks out the Trawler Skipper McPhee (George Summers) He is seen with a vast fishing fleet of trawlers and drifters, among these are:

LK.183 - Lerwick. *(Seen offshore during boat parliament scene)*
H.167 - Hull. *(Trawler with Andrew and Skipper McPhee)*
LT.133 - Lowestoft. *`Strive`.*
LT.231 - Lowestoft *`Merit`*
LT.1150 - Lowestoft.
LT.1156 - Lowestoft.
LT.1252 - Lowestoft.
LT.1297 - Lowestoft. *`Olivae`.*
IMJ.165 - Ijmuiden , Netherlands *`Golden Beam`*
BF.109 - Banff

Andrew (Niall MacGinnis) at Victoria Pier, Lerwick

Photo: BFI & Estate of Michael Powell

Left: The skipper of the `Vedra` Vernon `Black Jack` Sewell

Photos:
BFI & Estate of Michael Powell.

Two other trawlers are named but their registration numbers cannot be seen, they are : *`Mace`* and *`Sussex County`*. The *`Golden Beam`* can be seen in the storm sequence and moored alongside Victoria Pier.

POWELL`S ARK

Fifteen Shetland ponies were also taken to Foula and had to be off-loaded by barge. Of the ponies only a couple were harnessed, the rest were left to roam free and used later in the evacuation shots.

It was already decided early on that various animals would be needed in for some scenes, and these animals could not all be found on the Island. For instance several dogs were taken over for the Kirk scene and during the evacuation, one in particular, a Shetland Collie called Rab or Bob to the film crew. He ended up living at Elstree in the south of England with Bill Osborne after the movie was finished.

A trained eagle was also used in one of the opening shots as Mr Graham arrives on the Island. In the movie he blasts it with a shotgun, as it preys on a lamb, but obviously the owner got it back very much alive.

Top left:: Ponies being loaded on the Vedra. Left: Jimmy Henry struggles with ponies and a cow.

Photos:BFI & Estate of Michael Powell

Bob and the bird of prey

OTHER BOOKS BY THIS AUTHOR

THEIR FINAL MISSION
HELL ON HIGH GROUND
HELL ON HIGH GROUND 2
ALL IN A DAY`S WORK
AVRO ANSON UK HIGH GROUND CRASH LOG
MUDVILLE HEIGHTS
ALMOST HOME
L OST TO THE ISLES

HANOVER PUBLICATIONS